MW01015382

THE FEMININE
A MODE OF JOUISSANCE

MARIE-HÉLÈNE BROUSSE

THE FEMININE
A MODE OF JOUISSANCE

TRANSLATED BY
Janet Rachel

World Association of Psychoanalysis

Libretto series

First published in French by Navarin éditeur, Paris 6e, 2021

ISBN: 9798411660906

Lacanian Press
Publishing House of Lacanian Compass
New York, New York

Published with the support and collaboration of the World Association of Psychoanalysis for the *Libretto* series.

For more information:
www.lacaniancompass.com
lacanianpress@lacaniancompass.com

World Association of Psychoanalysis
www.wapol.org

Set in URW Baskerville type by Cyrus Saint Amand Poliakoff.

To Jacques-Alain Miller

The encounter with him was a tyché,

orienting my life towards and within psychoanalysis.

CONTENTS

A NEW WORLD?

Introduction to the English Edition

Psychoanalysis reveals that the feminine is not reducible to biological or cultural data. This book explores the feminine outside gender and beyond fantasy.

The first part is devoted to maternity, a function that is both biological and symbolic, and to the different values it takes on according to the subjective organization it comes to inhabit. I follow the thread of a remark made by Lacan during his seminar of 19 March 1974, wherein he predicted a rise in the power of the maternal function in the family, which had ceased to be patriarchal. It is titled "Voiding the Mother" because the mother blocks access to women.

The second part approaches the feminine via jouissance. Based on clinical data, the aim is to define a mode of jouissance that comes, in a way that is always unpredictable, as a supplement to the different jouissances affecting the speaking bodies that we are. This supplementary—not complementary—mode of jouissance does not correspond to a gendered classification. A schema is proposed.

If I were to characterize this second part, which I do in the title of this short introduction by taking inspiration from the title of Aldous Huxley's *Brave New World*, it would be a *Blank New World*. The American continent was and continues to be called the New World, and I propose to discover this new world that is potentially present inside everyone, whatever their gender.

Marie-Hélène Brousse

INTRODUCTION

Right now, women are making the news. This excitement on the world stage, particularly in the media, is not absent from what is being said in the psychoanalytic experience. But this modality of experience is different because in psychoanalysis every spoken word is singular, unique.

Current events are no longer just about demands for equality. Equality, as a universal value, has retained its power, but in new ways that are sometimes reduced to communitarian demands such as, "We want the same rights as them." Today's feminist movement asserts the particularity of women's experience beyond the rights they have already won—even if the right to abortion is still sometimes being questioned by reactionary currents. Ceasing to be oriented by the primacy of the masculine, a *sui generis* discourse is emerging that is focused on the experiences that women share amongst themselves. A new expression has thus appeared in our discourse which claims that a "mental load" weighs more heavily on women than on men.

By the same token, we can state that the man/woman binary, despite the fact that it is questioned in gender studies, still remains a signifying pair that continues to polarize discourses.

Psychoanalysis is also a discourse. But the Lacanian orientation emphasizes that, unlike other discourses, it excludes domination.[1] It displaces the element which is in the position of the agent of power in the three other discourses,[2] namely the master-word and prejudices in the master's discourse; exposed and objectified knowledge in the university discourse; and subjective division in the hysteric's discourse. Consequently, it does not rely on any of these established discourses, no more at the level of individuals than that of social groups. Lacanian orientated psychoanalysis puts libidinal objects in this place, revealing the power that these objects exert on the desire of each speaking being. This allows a deciphering to take place.

The psychoanalytic clinic sets out from the spoken words of analysands. What do they say today about women and the feminine? What has guided me in my research is precisely the fact that these two terms, "women" and "feminine," do not overlap.

The Feminine: A Mode of Jouissance

The feminine, traditionally assimilated to the maternal, is approached in contemporary discourse on the basis of gender, which multiplies the categories. Psychoanalytic

---

1. Cf. Lacan, J., "There Are Four Discourses" (1978), trans. A. R. Price with R. Grigg, *Culture/Clinic* 1, Minneapolis/London, University of Minnesota Press, 2013, pp. 3-4.

2. Lacan, J., *Seminar Book XVII, The Other Side of Psychoanalysis* (1969-1970), text established by J.-A. Miller, trans. R. Grigg, London/New York, Norton, 1991.

experience shows that gender is the result of identifications. Jouissance, however, does not respond to identifications.

In the 1970s, the feminist movements started with women demanding control over their bodies: family planning, contraception, legalization of abortion. All of these themes pointed in the direction of women appropriating their bodies and refusing to be assigned to the position of reproducer in procreation, a position that implied a destiny reduced to being mother and wife.

Today's feminism is different, as demonstrated by the #MeToo movement. This time it is a wave that emphasizes the demand that sexual jouissance no longer be defined by male desire alone. It stresses the particularity of women's sexuality and denounces their position as "victims"—a term which has become a master signifier in current affairs. Nevertheless, nothing in these statements calls into question the model, common to both men and women, of phallic jouissance. The spoken words of analysands, however, allow us to glimpse precisely another modality of jouissance in human beings.

Lacan considers that psychoanalysis cannot be practiced as such if the analyst "cannot meet at its horizon the subjectivity of his time."[3] He continues: "For how could he who knows nothing of the dialectic that engages him in a symbolic movement with so many lives possibly make his being the axis of those lives? Let him be well acquainted with the whorl into which his era draws him in the ongoing enterprise of Babel, and let him be aware of his function as an interpreter in the strife of languages."

3. Lacan, J., "The Function and Field of Speech and Language in Psychoanalysis" (1953), *Écrits*, trans. B. Fink, London/New York, Norton, 2006, p. 264.

For the analyst, it is a question of speaking the *lalangue* of each subject and of making interpretations based on the singularity of the subject.

It is, therefore, appropriate to be firmly committed to the following affirmation: in psychoanalysis, the approach to sex is singular. Each analysand is unique and his or her relation to sexual jouissance is determined neither by his or her biological sex, nor by gender, nor by the social order. It is determined by trauma. Sex is trauma: "The subject is there, in this obscure thing that sometimes we call trauma, or exquisite pleasure."[4]

By staying as close as possible to what is said in an analysis, to what is extracted from the statements of certain subjects that I hear as a psychoanalyst, to the always singular "well said" that we learn from, I propose to explore in this book what there is to say about the experiences of feminine jouissance in our time. I do not intend to look at it from all angles, still less to reduce it to being the equal of masculine jouissance, which always seems to be better defined and delineated. Lacan's advances are major insofar as feminine jouissance is concerned, precisely because he determines it from its very own mystery—non-localizable and unlimited. We draw upon this in our practice and in this present attempt at an elaboration.

4. Lacan, J., "Of Structure as an Inmixing of an Otherness Prerequisite to Any Subject Whatever," *The Lacanian Review* 12, 2021, p. 26.

Epistemic Encounter

Lacan always insisted that psychoanalysts should not isolate themselves but should open themselves up to neighboring disciplines. His teaching bears the trace of a constant interest in the different fields of knowledge which he continually puts at the service of the progress of psychoanalysis. Borrowed concepts, immersed in the analytic discourse, are given a specific definition and a new use. The resonances are numerous—it is invigorating.

A contingency of encounters as well as the sense of the necessity to link psychoanalysis with the current advances of science produced an opening for me. This is why I went to meet two quantum physicists: Catherine Pépin, researcher in theoretical physics at the CEA, and Matteo Barsuglia, researcher at the CNRS. *The Lacanian Review*[5] published these interviews, from which three terms emerged: the "void" and the "gravitational waves" of "black holes." These concepts have proven to be operative in the approach to the feminine jouissance of speaking bodies in analysis.

Researchers argue that the void that there is produces energy that unfolds along different pathways. Another element peculiar to quantum physics is not without interest for psychoanalysis of the Lacanian orientation: quantum objects are, at the same time, waves and particles. They can therefore be in two places at the same time. The qubits are, at one and the same time, 0 and 1. Our thesis is that by introducing what he calls the logic of sexuation,

5. Barsuglia, M., Brousse, M.-H. and Mabille, D., "The Real and the Metaphoric in Physics," and Brousse, M.-H., De Georges, P., and Pépin, C., "The Perfection of the Void", *The Lacanian Review* 7, Spring 2019, pp. 14-27 & 28-50.

Lacan makes it possible to affirm that speaking bodies can find themselves responding, at one and the same time, to a logic of the for-all and to one which he calls the logic of the not-all—a term we shall seek to specify from its manifestations in what analysands say.

The object *a*, invented by Lacan, is not a desired object, but rather an object that causes desire in humans. It is not grasped directly, but passes through what the analysand says, according to the waves it produces in speech. In the course of an analysis, these waves will reveal the black hole that is the experience of jouissance. Unconscious desire is a wave that can be grasped by the tracks it leaves in language.

The idea came to me to borrow these two notions, void and waves, and to put them to the test of analytic matter: the *motérialité* of the speaking body. *Motérialisme*, a neologism devised by Lacan, designates the "way in which language has been spoken and also heard as such, in its particularity." It is the word grasped as matter that is deposited: here "the unconscious takes hold."[6] The mathematical materiality of the void in physics finds an echo in the *motérialité* specific to *lalangue* proper to each speaking body in psychoanalysis.

This book, which is about feminine jouissance and not about women, is the fruit of this idea. Its two parts are articulated as follows. The first, "Voiding the Mother," starts from an equivocation of *lalangue* and endeavors to show that the current mutations of maternity (a symbolic

6. Lacan, J., "Geneva Lecture on the Symptom" (1975), trans. R. Grigg, *Analysis* 1, 1989, p. 14. [TN: Two neologisms: *lalangue* joins the article and the noun (thetongue), and *motérialisme* is a play on words between "*mot*" (word) and "materialism."]

function) are producing new paradoxes in what Lacan developed around the desire of the mother (which is not only symbolic). The second part, "The Void as the Feminine, a Mode of Jouissance," which is based on clinical elements collected during analyses of *parlêtres* (speaking beings) gendered as man as well as woman, offers a sketch of jouissance on the feminine side.

"Man and woman,
[…] are nothing but signifiers."

—JACQUES LACAN, *Encore*

VOIDING THE MOTHER

Traditionally the feminine is assimilated to the maternal in a confusion between woman and female. To have access to the feminine, it is necessary to make a separation from the mother. That is why I have called this first part "Voiding the Mother." Arising from an ambiguity, such as *Venus Anadyomene* ("Venus Rising from the Sea"), this expression leads us from waves to the void. Will you hear me out?

A CHILDHOOD MEMORY IN ANAMORPHOSIS

It is a first childhood memory, one that escapes parental narration—parents often recount to their children the first moments of their childhood. It is therefore neither a borrowed memory nor the parents' memory, but rather a memory of the subject in question that has been refined through the mechanism of analysis.

On the beach in Cannes in June, on holiday with my parents, I was very busy. My mother was pregnant with my brother, so I was two and a half years old. In my memory, she stood with my father at her side, under an umbrella, some distance from the sea. I had a small bucket with a handle. During those ten days of vacation, I spent my time going back and forth between the shore and my mother's feet. It was a serious business. I filled my bucket with sea water and then emptied it at my mother's feet. I had a clear and self-formulated goal: I will empty the sea [*vider la mer*]. I did this without ever tiring during the whole time we spent at the beach. I had no doubt that I could do it. But I have no recollection whatsoever of my leaving—in other words, there is a refusal to acknowledge the failure of the project.

I will add a supplementary element of infantile neurosis: I had a phobia of algae and other elements floating underwater, a phobia that gradually subsided.

Emptying the sea, voiding the mother[1] of the child she was carrying—this little invisible and living algae—that was the objective.

At this point in my life, I can see that if I did not then notice my failure to "empty the sea/void the mother," it is because I never stopped trying to do just that! My first Master's thesis in the Department of Psychoanalysis at the University of Paris 8 dealt with the discourse addressed by the medical hygienists to the nurses whose leitmotiv was, "Woman was born to be a mother," followed by my doctoral thesis on "The Mother-Child Relationship: A Psychoanalyst's Fantasy," in which I contrasted Lacan's teaching with the currents in post-Freudian thinking that

1. [TN: In French there is a direct equivocation between the words for *sea* and *mother* which is not evident in English: *mer/mère*. And in French, the word *vider* can stand for both "to empty" and "to void," hence: "*Vider la mer, vider la mère*."]

were drifting from father to mother. Finally, a difficulty encountered in the direction of the analyses that I was conducting led me to write a Lacanian-oriented reinterpretation of the mother-daughter *ravage*. I showed there that the analytic cure of certain subjects met with a stumbling block caused by the orientation given by Freud as a consequence of the confused concept of *Penisneid.* It was more appropriate to start from the concept of *privation*, as Lacan deployed it in different seminars, thus differentiating it from castration and frustration. This privation is to be put in relation to an "insult": a language event leaving a mark on the body, since it names an experience of jouissance in the speaking body.

Today, as I put this trajectory into perspective, I look back, and this backward glance produces an anamorphosis. What I see is an attempt to dissociate the desire of the analyst from the desire of the mother. This anamorphosis makes it possible for me to put an end to this "*vider la mèr(e)*." How? It is simply a matter of moving the coordinates. This is now possible for me for a number of reasons.

The first is a reading oriented by the different moments of Lacan's teaching on the mother, all the way up to the later Lacan. Reading Lacan takes time; each reading brings forth new flashes, is a discovery, a new encounter.

The second is the importance of Jacques-Alain Miller's many contributions on the woman-mother binary. Amongst them, two short texts—one from 1992 titled "Médée à mi-dire," the other following in 1994—are particularly enlightening. They allow a reduction to the bone of this binary: "Let's go all the way: a real woman is always Medea [...] Medea is there to show us what happens when the 'of the woman' lurking in the mother bursts out—when the logic of the signifier 'woman' prevails over 'mother'."[2] And he concludes (in 1994) by qualifying as "labyrinthine" the "response to the question of the choice to be made between mother and woman."[3]

But later, in 2006-2008, J.-A. Miller made an innovative advance from another angle, this time not in relation to the mother-woman binary, but to the place of the analyst in the cure. He formalized, among other things, a new definition of the symptom and, on 11 June 2008, he identified the place of the analyst as "the place of *plus personne*," the place of no-one-anymore.[4] This resonated in me with the notion of void, in the context of an encounter, which I shall go on to mention.

The third reason is linked to this innovation. It seemed to me that since the encounter between J.-A. Miller and Jean-Pierre Changeux[5] on the advances in biology, our working community had still not taken note of the progress of the hard sciences, such as physics. I recently had the opportunity to meet and interview

---

2. Miller, J.-A., "Médée à mi-dire" (1992), *La Cause du désir* 89, March 2015, p. 114.

3. Miller, J.-A., "Mèrefemme" (1994), *La Cause du désir* 89, *op. cit.*, p. 122.

4. Miller, J.-A., "L'orientation lacanienne: Tout le monde est fou" (2007-2008), teaching delivered within the framework of the Department of Psychoanalysis at the University of Paris 8, lesson of 11 June 2008 (unpublished). See also, lesson from 4 June 2008, published in English as "Everyone Is Mad", *Culture/Clinic* 1, University of Minnesota Press, 2013, p. 20.

5. Cf. Changeux, J.-P., "*L'Homme neuronal*, entretien avec J. Bergès, A. Grosrichard, É. Laurent & J.-A. Miller, *Ornicar ?* 17/18, Spring 1979, pp. 137-174; republished 2020 (Paris, Navarin).

important researchers in the field of quantum physics. This allowed me to borrow the concepts of the void, the black hole and gravitational waves—useful concepts for the field of psychoanalysis. The fundamental state of the elementary particles of matter is the quantum vacuum, which contains neither movement nor entropy. This void of matter is and remains a mass of energy [*plein d'énergie*]. Therefore, there exists an energy of the void.

As a result, this ever-failing attempt to void the mother received further clarification. What is the void outside the "there is no" (as in no child in the womb of the mother)? What is *the void that there is*?

LACANIAN ADVANCES

In his approach to the mother-child bond, Lacan activates a radical change of perspective at the level of structure, topology, and logic.

Structure

Lacan moves from an approach determined by the chronology of the bond to an approach based on structure. It is not that he does not take time and development into account, and his early texts, "Family Complexes"[6] and "The Mirror Stage,"[7] bear witness to this. But even

6. Lacan, J., "The Family Complexes" (1938), trans. A. Khan, *Critical Texts* 5:3, 1988.

7. Lacan J., "The Mirror Stage as Formative of the I Function as Revealed in Psychoanalytic Experience" (1949), trans. B. Fink, *Écrits: The First Complete Edition in English*, London/New York, Norton, 2006, pp. 75-81.

then, the family as structure prevails over a chronology of development in the formalization of the mother-child bond it produces.

Topology

This first change subsequently gives rise to a second, topological change. Lacan passes from an inside-out, interior-exterior, container-content, surface-depth topology to one that allows a major change of dimension.

All of these binaries are in fact borrowed from the dimension of the imaginary and rely on the image of the body that is imposed by the perception of the body itself. The dominance of this image, however, leads to the bag of skin and the sphere. Lacan reminds us of this: "Analysis only ever apprehends the body as what is most imaginary […] We apprehend it as a form […] through its appearance […] Then, he saw this body, he abstracted it, he he made it into a sphere: the good form. That reflects a bubble, a bag of skin. Beyond this idea of the enveloped and the enveloping sac."[8] Melanie Klein radicalized this formula in her theory of the mother's body as a large container of heterogeneous objects. By contrast, as early as "Family Complexes," Lacan makes it clear that he places weaning as trauma not on the side of the child, but on that of the mother. In the same way in *Seminar X, Anxiety*, the dividing line passes between the mother on one side and the placenta attributed to the child on the

8. Lacan. J., "MIT Lecture on Topology, 2 December 1975," trans. J.W. Stone and R. Grigg, *The Lacanian Review* 12, 2021, p. 79.

other.[9] At the moment of what is commonly called the mirror stage, the two partners involved, we might say, are the original fragmented body and the image in the mirror, which is the first other of identification; the mother is not immediately part of the scene. All these examples show, as Lacan points out, that, "Beyond this idea of the enveloped and the enveloping sac (man started out with this), the idea of the concentricity of the spheres [,] we must apprehend something of another order than spherical space."[10]

This Lacanian orientation tends to give way to a Moebian topology. The mother-child relationship can then be envisaged with the help of the topological objects developed by Lacan from the seminar "Identification": cross-cap, projective plane, interior eight, interior and exterior torus, Moebius strip.[11] In the lesson of 30 May 1962, Lacan proposes to inscribe in a torus the difference between the void and nothingness, nothingness being of the order of the object.

Logic

The third change is based on logic and finds its fulfilment in Chapters 6 and 7 of *Seminar XX*, *Encore*. Using the terms chosen by Lacan himself in 1972-73, it is customary to speak of the masculine and feminine sides of the table of sexuation.[12] In so doing, there is a risk of spontaneously

---

9. Cf. Lacan J., *Seminar Book X, Anxiety* (1962-1963), text established by J.-A. Miller, trans. A.R. Price, Cambridge, Polity, 2014, p. 167.

10. Lacan. J., "MIT Lecture on Topology", *op. cit.*.

11. Cf. Lacan, J., Le Séminaire, livre IX, "L'identification" (1961-1962), lesson of 30 May 1962, unpublished.

12. Cf. Lacan, J., *Seminar Book XX, Encore* (1972-1973), text established by J.-A. Miller, trans. B. Fink, London/New York, Norton, 1998, p. 78,

falling back into the discourse of the master. Yet at the beating heart of the analytic discourse, the terms "masculine" and "feminine," as put forward by Lacan, refer neither to gender nor to biology.

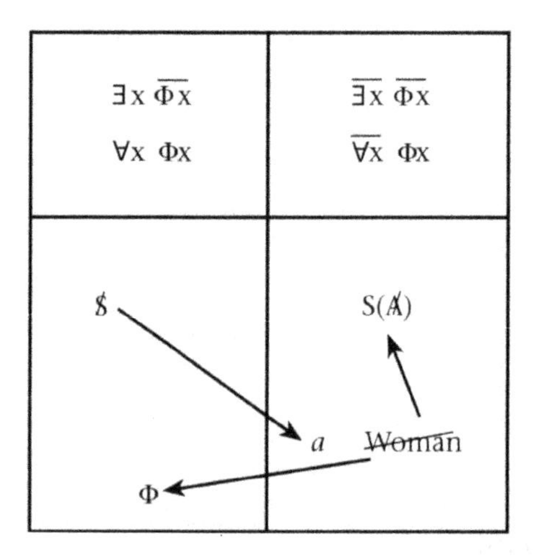

Lacan makes it clear: "Let us approach things from the pole at which every x is a function of Φ, that is, from the pole where man is situated. One ultimately situates oneself there by choice—women are free to situate themselves there if it pleases them to do so."[13] Or again, "one is not obliged, when one is male, to situate oneself on the side of $\forall x\, \Phi x$. One can also situate oneself on the side of the not-all."[14] Indeed, from the outset he stated that because of the fact that we inhabit language, the semblant is in power and the semblant is not meaning. Sex as a

reproduced here.

13. *Ibid.*, p. 71.

14. *Ibid.*, p. 76.

modality of jouissance is not a matter of identification, but of an act, of a choice. It is the sexual act, there where there is no sexual relation.

In presenting the table of sexuation, Lacan calls for "caution" regarding meaning, which is always sexual. Let us therefore be attentive to his formulations: "We'll start with the four propositional formulas at the top of the table, two of which lie to the left, the other two to the right. Every speaking being situates itself on one side or the other"[15]; "Those are the only possible definitions of the so-called man or woman portion for that which finds itself in the position of inhabiting language" (let's emphasize this "so-called"); on the other side, "you have the inscription of the woman portion of speaking beings. Any speaking being whatsoever, as is expressly formulated in Freudian theory, whether provided with the attributes of masculinity—attributes that remain to be determined—or not, is allowed to inscribe itself in this part." Let us note this non-gendered universalist formulation: "To any speaking being." And also, let us note this remark on the indeterminacy of what he qualifies as "attributes of masculinity." The organs do not function as reference points in sexuation; they are subject to the semblant and to a logic of the Φ function which is none other than castration inasmuch as it is the result of language and speech on the body and objects. It affects the entire body inasmuch as it is a speaking body.

Since the 1970s, nearly fifty years have passed. The master's discourse, traditionally organized by the binary "man-woman," has been transformed. In *Seminar VIII, Transference*, Lacan evokes the dialectic between neurosis

15. *Ibid.*, p. 79, et seq.

and perversion, the latter imposing, little by little, its modes of jouissance on the current discourse. I detect in it an intuition of what he will later develop by equivocating on the *père-version*[16], which is to say, other, new versions of the function formerly corresponding to the patriarch.

THE FAMILY IN THE TIME OF THE ONES-ALL-ALONE

In fifty years, this change has become an ambient reality. The concept of gender has gradually shattered the classic male/female binary into a multiplicity of signifiers proposed for identification. The identification process itself has changed. Gender identification used to be imposed by the family order. Today, the Name-of-the-Father has lost its power and everyone thinks they speak in their own name.

Lacan anticipated this when, in 1968, he mentioned the "evaporation" of the father: "I believe that in our day and age, we could classify the mark, the scar, left by the father's disappearance under the heading and general notion of *segregation*."[17] We are now dealing with Ones-all-alone,[18] speaking subjects who wish to self-identify

16. Lacan, J., *Seminar Book* XXIII, *The Sinthome* (1975-1976), text established by J.-A. Miller, trans. A.R. Price, Cambridge, Polity, 2016, p. 9 ("*version vers le père*, a version towards the father") & 130 ("How far does *père*-version extend? You know how I spell it."); cf. Seminar XXII, "R.S.I." (1974-1975), lesson of 21 January 1975, *Ornicar ?* 3, May 1975, pp. 104-110.

17. Lacan, J., "Note on the Father and Universalism" (1968), trans. R. Grigg, *The Lacanian Review* 3, 2017, p. 11.

18. According to the expression coined by Jacques-Alain Miller, "The Lacanian orientation. L'Un-tout-seul" (2010-2011), a lecture delivered within the framework of the Department of Psychoanalysis at the University of Paris 8 (unpublished).

according to a certainty which they judge to be intimate. But to do so, they resort to the categories of the modern master's discourse, which has exploded what used to be an S_1–S_2 (male/female) binary into an increasing series of multiple gendered positions. L, G, B, T, Q, intra, infra, inter… so many juxtaposable categories that reign today in international discourse. This is the reign of the phallic function—by which we mean the impact of language on the body that defines any speaking body.

As early as March 1973, Lacan introduced a new approach to sex based on logic. The side called "masculine"—the left side of the table of sexuation—concerns human bodies in as much as they speak, regardless of the gendered category with which they identify and according to which they are named. Let us call these speaking bodies "LOM", a neologism (homophonous with *l'homme*, "man") invented by Lacan to designate the impact of *having a body* on the subject of the unconscious.[19]

As for the "feminine" side, which is not the monopoly of the LOM we call "woman", it is no doubt sufficient to name it as "supplementary."[20] I propose "not-all-LOM."

The contemporary transformations of the family order are to be found on the LOM side. Because the sexual relation cannot be written, it is replaced in speaking beings by the social bond, a relationship that can be written in different ways via the family order between ascendants and descendants. The structures of kinship list the different variations. Consequently, as Lacan states, "The Mother remains the contaminator of woman for

19. Cf. Lacan, J., "Joyce the Symptom" (1975), trans. A.R. Price, *The Lacanian Review* 5, 2018, p. 13.

20. Lacan, J., *Seminar* XX, *Encore*, *op. cit.*, p. 73.

man's offspring."[21] The mother is traditionally defined by the care function perceived as a result of pregnancy. This is obviously far from always being the case in reality. But it is a semblant that creates, per se, part of the real. Not only do we have at our disposal what the mother is, or was, for the child, that the analysand is or has been, but we also receive mothers in analysis. Among them, today, some are "gendered" men. Each one produces a version of what "being a mother" is for her, her singular version of the difficulties, as well as the delights, of motherhood. Mothers are therefore LOMs like the others, all the more so in today's family where father and mother have become undifferentiated.

Undifferentiation

If in the past the symbolic order differentiated the Father function from the Mother function, today the term "parent" condenses it. "Parenthood" is the new signifier! LOMs are parents, undifferentiated in a function that is unique in current legal discourse in our societies. In this unique function of parent, care takes precedence over authority and name. The assignment of gender—masculine for the father and feminine for the mother—that used to be covered by the semblants of the family order, has faded away.

It is clear that the term "father" has never been equated with "progenitor." Even today, while science can trace the progenitor, there is no overlap between these two

---

21. Lacan, J., "Television" (1973), trans. D. Hollier, R. Krauss and A. Michelson, in *Television: A Challenge to the Psychoanalytic Establishment*, ed. J. Copjec, London/New York, Norton, 1990, pp. 3-46.

words. The difference between father and progenitor has, paradoxically, become even clearer. "Father" refers to the symbolic order and not to reproduction. To a lesser extent, the same applies to the mother. Freud had already noted this in his article on Leonardo da Vinci and his two mothers.[22] Nowadays, reproduction and care take first place. In many countries, traditional corporal punishment is prohibited. The relation to the child's body is regulated by law; the law has replaced the paternal authority over mother and child.

The center of gravity of the family, defined by this new trio—the child, his or her mother(s) and the law—has shifted towards the child. We are in the time of the iron order of the social, as Lacan said in his seminar "*Les non-dupes errent*."[23]

An Unintended Consequence: Exit the Mother

The movement that is spreading in the twenty-first century within the dominant discourse has, in the end, not extended the domain of mothers. Certainly, at the outset, it might have seemed that the axiom, "All LOMs are mothers" would become a new universal and that we would witness the extension of the domain of mothers, or even the reduction of the family to the mother-child bond.

---

22. Cf. Freud, S., "Leonardo Da Vinci and a Memory of His Childhood" (1910), *SE* 11, pp. 59-138.

23. Cf. Lacan, J., Seminar XXI, "Les non-dupes errent" (1973-1974), lesson of 19 March 1974 (unpublished), "There is something whose effect I should like to point out [...] It's quite strange that here the social takes on the prevalence of a knot, which literally weaves the fabric of so many existences, [...] restoring to itself an order cast in iron."

For Freud, love for the father was foundational to the subject and to the Name. Lacan reduces the Oedipus complex to the paternal metaphor: the Name-of-the-Father as a principle of linguistic organization in the symbolic order, with the desire of the mother opening, beyond the child, to an *x*, an "unknown" in the mathematical sense of the term. With the fading of the paternal function, i.e. the loss of love for the Father and the decline of the paternal metaphor, a new alternative emerged. In 1974, Lacan notes that a new function had appeared, the one he calls the "naming function,"[24] and added that "the mother is sufficient [...] to designate the project, to trace it, to indicate its path." Today, this function takes precedence over "what there is of the Name-of-the-Father." What results from this passage of the Mother to primary place is a progressive transformation of Fathers into Mothers. The social aspect of a function has been substituted for the name. It has established the social in place of the familial and a new order that is no less ironclad. This has now come to pass.

But this transformation or displacement of name to function, which, it seems, should have produced an extension of the power of mothers, has had an unintended consequence. Once the Fathers were replaced by the Mothers, the latter, in turn, were replaced by the term "parent," a term taking over mothers, as such. Secondly, in the twenty-first century, the parent has made it possible to do away with the mother: the mother has been voided!

Let us follow Lacan's indication that there where the paternal metaphor was, a knotting has emerged.[25]

---

24. *Ibid., et seq.*

25. Cf. *Ibid.*

Metaphor is a function of substitution of one signifier for another in a signifying chain, producing an effect of meaning. The substitution of the desire of the mother for the Name-of-the-Father organized a familial order. It thus involved the binary of two signifiers, "father" and "mother," to which other signifiers were attached. The meaning obtained from this metaphorical drift articulated desire to law via this initial pair S_1–S_2, catching and resorbing jouissance in the phallic function.

Two modifications should be noted. The first one concerns nomination: function has replaced nomination in the time of the Ones-all-alone. Function is not transmitted by the familial order, unlike the name. The Ones-all-alone are without lineage.

The second modification concerns metaphor, which lost its hitherto dominant role in symbolic functioning to the benefit of the image. The empire of the image is constantly being increased by new technologies via the multiplication of screens. As Gérard Wajcman argues, the gaze has become central to the social bond. "Omnivoyance" and, consequently, metonymy and proximity have come in the place of the signifying chain.[26] J.-A. Miller, analyzing the modality of the tweet,[27] demonstrated the consequences for the social bond, and therefore for discourse, of the passage to a rhetoric of "short forms" demanded by this type of media. Advertising campaigns play on this same rhetoric of brevity, with a surprising and punchy effect. We have moved from "demonstration" to "monstration."

26. Cf. Wajcman, G., *L'Œil absolu*, Paris, Denoël, 2010.

27. Cf. Miller, J.-A., "Bourdin, l'Homme pulsionnel", *Lacan Quotidien* 485, 6 March 2015, available online at lacanquotidien.fr

Correlatively, the discourse about the child has changed. The child has become a person in his own right. He, too, is taken as One-all-alone, no matter how many brothers and sisters he has. He no longer merely embodies lineage, where he was classified as a sibling according to an ordinal calculation; considering children as Ones-all-alone implies that every child is an only child.

The child thus becomes a fellow human, a peer, and a subject of law with rights. He is assumed to have knowledge from the outset. The child, however, remains an object *a*. He catches our eye from the first three-dimensional ultrasound scan; the sound of his heartbeat functions as a voice. Still in the womb, he is already the object of procedures, preventive detections, even surgical operations. An object for the reproductive sciences, he is also an object for the social. While a child has always been a commodity in patriarchal societies, now he has become a commodity that can be bought. Some medically assisted reproduction units publish this as a manufacturing specialty: "We take care of everything, all you have to do is choose the color of the eyes!"

From Chain to Knotting: The Three'd of the Iron Order

In the Seminar "*Les non-dupes errent*," after having affirmed the passage from "the name" to "nominate to" [*nommer à*], Lacan deploys this passage from the coupling by two towards a knotting with three. This passage from the model of the chain to the model of the Borromean knot leads him to specify another model more capable of formalizing the effects of the replacement of the familial by the social. He emphasizes that the "social" at work in the *nommer à* function—the function of *nominating to*—is the "trace" of a return, in the real, of the Name-of-the-Father that is foreclosed in the symbolic. And he asks, "What is this trace, designated as the return of the Name-of-the-Father in the real, since the Name-of-the-Father is precisely *verworfen*, foreclosed, rejected?"[28] In other words, why are we not all psychotic? Furthermore, why has this distinction between neurosis and psychosis become obsolete in discourse today?

He then introduces the term ex-sistence, which characterizes the real. And he goes on to say, "If something ex-sists to something, it means precisely that it is not coupled to it—it is *three'd* to it, if you'll allow me this neologism."

This foreclosure of the name brings the real to the forefront and makes the parental couple, archetype of the symbolic dimension, move to the *nouage à trois*, to the knotting of three, which is the order of the real. The knot is what allows us to escape from the madness that would otherwise be there to meet us. It ex-sists, but is not demonstrable—it shows. It shows that, as a subject, "what possesses us is nothing but a desire and, moreover, desire of the Other, a desire by which we are, from the start, alienated." And the knot itself bears on that which "has zero essence." We are simply "stuck, squeezed into a certain knot", which ex-sists us. This knot, which organizes the nomination to a function, and no longer the belonging to lineages, is not a form of metaphor or, for that matter, of metonymy.

The time that has passed since 1974 has allowed us to slightly modify what Lacan anticipated. In this foreclosure of the Father that is the *nomination to*, it is no more

---

28. Lacan, J., Le Séminaire, livre XXI, "Les non-dupes errent", *op. cit. et seq.*

a question of mother or father, but simply of "parent", a contemporary term. The passage from the foreclosed Name-of-the-Father to the *nomination to* that orders the social requires (in order for the desire of the Other to subsist in the subject) that it repose directly on the real of something that ex-sists in the subject.

In the era of foreclosure, speaking beings are *three'd*. Lacan points out that "everything that makes a knot ex-sists us." The knot between three *ex-sistants*, between these three reals—"as the real itself is three"—"jouissance, the body and death," is what traps the speaking being. The function of *nomination to* allows a single parent to situate the child in this new iron order, that is to say real and not symbolic. This knot thus makes it possible to "designate the project", "make the trace", "indicate the path" from the social to the child.

We therefore arrive at the following observation: This new iron order, just as it has abolished fathers, has done away with mothers. Where a victory for mothers was expected, we are witnessing the victory of a hybrid, "the parent," a LOM that abolishes all difference, be it natural or gendered, hierarchical or egalitarian. The discourse of our time has voided the mother of the family in favor of the *parent-all-alone* of a *child-all-alone*. And the transmission process itself has changed. The family and the signifying chain have been replaced by the knotting of the order of the real, ex-sisting the symbolic and the imaginary and transforming them in the process. The Ones-all-alone are *three'd*—the three'd of the iron order.

Lacan, in the lesson of his Seminar that I am citing, distinguishes three formulations: "To make the trace of it, to designate the project, and to show the way to it." These three formulations characterize the parent at the time of the Ones-all-alone: "trace," of the family and the name, written on the body in the real; "project," taking the place of the desire of the Other in the symbolic; "path," all made of virtualities and indicated by the image.

THREE CLINICAL LESSONS

With psychoanalysis, however, we listen to analysands who use all the signifiers made available to them by the archaeological strata of discourse of which they are the effect: parents, father, mother, grandfather, grandmother, brother, sister. What do they say?

As Lacan noted during one of his lectures in the United States in 1975, "We see, as Freud tells us, people irresistibly talking to us about their mom and dad. Whereas the only instruction we give them is simply to say what they... I would not say what they think, but what they think they think."[29] In spite of the modifications that I have just mentioned about this mutation of discourse through the deployment of the Ones-all-alone, what Lacan said in 1975 remains valid in 2020 in the space of the analytic sessions. How is this possible? Each analysand, since the beginnings of psychoanalysis, is unique. In clinical practice, any generalization comes up against this absolute singularity, whether it concerns the problem or the solution. We can therefore only speak of inflections in the analysand's discourse and of observable recurrences in the strategies of demand and desire. Three clinical vignettes shed light on this change.

---

29. Lacan, J., "Yale University, Kanzer Seminar, 24 November 1975," trans. Philip Dravers, *The Lacanian Review* 12, 2021: 35-57

*

A man in a couple with another man wanted to have children. Thanks to a surrogate mother in a foreign country, he managed to have two, very desired children. His partner, although less certain than he was, accepted. The man established a caring relationship with the mother, who was both the donor and the carrier, and he looked after her when she had an accident after the births. Before each birth, he travelled abroad for several months with his own mother to pick up the children, declare them under French law and obtain the necessary identity papers—not without difficulty. His companion also went with him, but on a more occasional basis. Family life ensued: a couple of two men, two little girls, a grandmother. During a session, the man wondered about his position in the family, complaining that his job was more demanding than his companion's, and that when he arrived home he always had to put his daughters' lives in order. His companion was "lax," "yielding to the slightest request from the girls," and he found himself having to give the commands. He would have preferred to have a different position. His dissatisfaction connotes his structure. His companion, who was much more present at home and less interested in sex, did not complain about the girls. He took care of them "obeying their whims." Two parents, therefore, rather satisfied with life, and two little girls who are well adapted to school, curious, and demanding much attention. A rather ordinary family, after all. But who is the father, who is the mother? Neither of them? Or both of them?

An analysand came for analysis driven by the discord that had arisen between her and her girlfriend. They had two children. Her partner bore the first, a son that she claimed as her own, and the analysand bore the second, a daughter; her partner also considered herself to be that child's mother. Both children were from anonymous sperm donors. The bond between the parents had ceased to be satisfactory at all levels—sexual, economic and emotional. In short, there was disenchantment and blame. They were not married and the breakup was all the more difficult as the law was not involved. Nevertheless, the law will eventually be convened, and the break-up will take a while to find an agreement. When it was finally obtained, each one took back the child she had given birth to. Both children played an important role in the agreement, and neither of them repudiated the two *mother-fathers*. Each called themselves the child of both and demanded to move from one home to the other, like any child of separated couples. They were forced to start with a system of alternation, and as they grew older they moved towards a more flexible system. The modality was different, but the analysand found herself in the same rather paternal place (in the classical sense of the term) in her relation to both her daughter and her son. Today, she has left behind her reproaches and complaints. Her love for her children is quite simple. In her sessions, she speaks about another modality of her desire—about desiring beyond the parent that she is.

Another young woman had just become a mother. Her husband, whom she had met a few years earlier in circumstances where she had been unfaithful, was a rather traditional man. The fact that she chose him for this was due to her subjective coordinates, with a deficit on the side of her father. Her husband had the same university education and the same degree as her. They both worked in the same industry. They were similar, with a tendency to rivalry. The marriage ceremony was traditional; he wanted her to adopt her married name as her customary name. Hesitation Waltz... The decisive argument, among other conscious rationalizations and unconscious determinations, was that she wished to bear the same patronym as her future children. The couple then wanted a child, and a year later the child was born. Straight away she established a balanced bond with her child. She went back to work. Her husband told her that since she became a mother she has been bossing him around. But she was faced with his inactivity around the home: he no longer did any housework, and did not get up at night when the child cried, even if she woke him up to ask him to. In short, the mother she had become was in conflict with her man, whose lack of sexual desire she also complained about. The "mental load," as well as the housework and errands, deprived her of the education she wanted to pursue. She was divided between being a modern LOM and holding the traditional position of mother to which she found herself assigned. She was torn. But she demanded equality between the parents with regard to the care of the child and domestic chores, in the name of a desire that took her beyond the family.

*

These three clinical scenarios highlight a few elements. The first is that, even in these new modalities of the family, it is necessary to make an essential difference between the paternal function and the dad. Freud had made this distinction, and Lacan had done so even more clearly. I remember a little boy who said to me, "I have to tell you that my daddy is my father." He had understood something essential. We know that Lacan, on two occasions, stresses that when a father identifies himself with the paternal function as such, the consequence is catastrophic for the structural organization of the child. Is it the same for the maternal function? It is different, but the consequences of the mother's absence of desire, to be understood as a desire that does not concern the child but goes beyond him, are no less catastrophic. If the *nomination to* comes in place of the link between naming and desire, it does not abolish, for the child, the alienation-separation dialectic necessary for the speaking body. It emphasizes the parent, who, like the child, is subject to division and to the want-to-be that no identification can resolve.

The analytic clinic also teaches us that parents who are of the same biological sex, and who are determined by the choice of what they suppose is the same gender, are, as far as the unconscious is concerned, subject to the same regulations of drive and desire as all LOMs, i.e. the castration function operated by language. The choice of jouissance that they display has little to do with the determination that the mark of jouissance operates in them—what Freud called the unary trait—produced in their flesh by a contingent and random encounter in the order of *lalangue*. In an analytic trajectory, by way of an equivocation, it can emerge as a surprise.

On the other hand, it is clear that the analytic clinic has not been able to keep to classifications, going outside this framework (supported as it is by the function of nomination, in terms of neurosis, psychosis or perversion) in order to adopt the Borromean perspective, which makes the *sinthome* the new name of the knot for the *three'd* Ones-all-alone. In *Seminar VIII, Transference*, Lacan shows that Freud anticipated this very early on in one of his "Papers on Technique": It is a question of "taking advantage of the opening up of the unconscious, because soon it will have found another trick."[30] The unconscious is a voracious fish that snaps up all the innovations of discourse.

What can we say about this desire of the mother, to use the classic formulation, or about this desire of the LOM parent? First of all, that it is underpinned by the function **Φ**, coextensive with the universality of subjective division, and thus transforms part of real jouissance into phallic jouissance, circulating in the speaking body. Desire, outside meaning, takes possession of the body via the window of the fantasy. The parent's desire, of course, invests the child, for better or for worse, but it does not stop there and aims at a point beyond the child. This point of chronic dissatisfaction, which stems from the difference between the object that causes desire and the desired object,[31] constructs a void that is also a key space for the child subject.

What is this vanishing point for LOM parents? In the sessions of *Seminar VI* which he devoted to *Hamlet* in 1959, Lacan made it clear that for Hamlet's mother, the vanishing point of the paternal order is her woman's desire. Today I would say that the vanishing point of the parent's desire is the feminine, regardless of the sex or gender by which the parent self-identifies—the feminine, or "of the feminine," and not the women. It is obvious that the feminine does not necessarily coincide with the organism or gender.

---

30. Lacan, J., *Seminar VIII, Transference* (1960-1961), text established by J.-A. Miller, trans. B. Fink, Cambridge, Polity, 2015, p. 334.

31. Lacan, J., *Seminar X, Anxiety* (1962-1963), *op. cit.*, pp. 90-93

THE VOID THAT THERE IS

The iron order of the social has thus managed to achieve what the child on the beach, unwittingly playing on the equivocation of her language, failed to do with a bucket—and that was left hanging until the choice of psychoanalysis. *Emptying so that there is no more* always turns into a remainder. The barrel that the Danaids emptied was eternally full. Voiding the mother who is no longer there produced an avatar, a mutant, the parent.

But nothing allows this emptying to reach the void that there is. Our hypothesis is that, supplementary to the LOM side, *the void that there is* is one possible definition of the feminine.

François Cheng recounts a conversation with Lacan: "It remains for me to evoke that day (in 1977) devoted to work in his country house, a clear day when the high summer had the flavor of eternity. In the evening, in the vast room gilded by the rays of the setting sun, in response to a question he had asked, I began, encouraged as I was by his attentive silence, to speak of my life, my experiences of Beauty and Hell, of Exile and of Double tongue. I can still see his face suddenly lighting up with a smile full of mischief and kindness when he said to me: '*You see, our job is to demonstrate the impossibility of living, so that we can make life a little possible. You've experienced the extreme gap—why not expand it even further to the point of identifying with it? You who have the wisdom to understand that the Void is Breath and that Breath is Metamorphosis, you will not stop until you have given free rein to the Breath that remains to you, a writing, why not exhaust it!*' With these words we parted."[32] Writing, like poetry, implies the Void.

---

32. "François Cheng et Jacques Lacan", *L'Âne* 4, February-March 1982. Maria-Josefina Fuentes sent me this extract, which is available online.

The void is different from nothing, if we follow the inspiration given by conceptual innovations in the field of quantum physics, this plays out in the position of the analyst.

When Lacan, in one of his last texts, returns to the four discourses, he emphasizes that three of them are discourses of domination, and that only the analytic discourse is an exception. Science has modified the master's discourse and has increased its powers by means of algorithms; the hysteric's discourse has conquered the social field; and the university discourse reigns over knowledge. The analytic discourse has vanished each time it has tried to dominate. In analyses, it is obvious that any attempt to influence the analysand is immediately doomed to failure. The structure of analytic discourse and the conditions of its effectiveness exclude that.

The place of the analyst is tenable only on the condition of being devoid of all subjectivity. This condition therefore implies a particular emptiness. In his teaching, J.-A. Miller shows its causes and consequences when he develops the idea that, "*a* is nothing"[33]—an affirmative and non-negative formulation on the one hand, and "the place of no-one-anymore" on the other, that indicates an active void.

The desire of the analyst, a formula invented by Lacan in order to separate this desire from the counter-transference, finds, in the orientation developed by J.-A. Miller, a new definition starting out from the body

---

33. Miller J.-A., "L'orientation lacanienne: Le tout dernier Lacan" (2006-2007), teaching delivered within the framework of the Department of Psychoanalysis at the University of Paris 8, lesson of 9 May 2007, unpublished.

of the analyst in flesh and blood, and no longer only from his interpretations. Interpretations, moreover, are today oriented towards the explosion of meaning arising from equivocation: it is equivocation that puts sound material, and therefore the body of language, to work. Analysis thus implies a void which is not nothing, but is void of meaning.

The place of the analyst mobilizes a void of meaning that becomes a mass of energy: it is desire outside meaning, but not outside the body.

"Women say nothing."

—JACQUES LACAN, *R.S.I.*

"Castration is the secret of the visual field...
This is the secret that gives radiance to the works
that conceal or, more precisely, that deny castration."

—JACQUES-ALAIN MILLER, "The Lost Object of
Language," *The Lacanian Review* 8 (2019)

THE FEMININE: THE VOID AS A MODE OF JOUISSANCE

In 1972-1973, in his Seminar *Encore*, Lacan approaches sexuality in a way that is unprecedented outside the field of psychoanalysis—and even within it. In fact, this advance implies a decoupling from the discourse that controls us.

One of the traditional organizers of the master's discourse is the woman/man binary, made legitimate until recently by a supposed order of Nature. Paradoxically, this binary has seen its power further strengthened since the beginning of the twenty-first century by the political affirmation of gender studies. It is based on both the imaginary and the symbolic: the global image of the body and the minimal symbolic structure, S_1-S_2. In speaking beings, it helps to supplement, by way of the social bond, the sexual relation that does not exist, made impossible by language. The traditional hierarchies of function and power identified the Name with the paternal function and the social order with the family order. The current claims on filiation, on the other hand, are derived from the aspirations of the Ones-all-alone and proceed by means of auto-nomination, relying on the possibilities opened up by the collaboration of the capitalist discourse with the advances of science.

CONCERNING A FEMININE POSITION OF SPEAKING BODIES

The fact that "man and woman should be there at the outset is first and foremost a matter of language,"[1] says Lacan in, *...or Worse*. And, he continues in *Le moment de conclure*, "Sex, as I told you, is an act of saying."[2] Sex does not depend on the image of the body, or on anatomy, or on gender. What Lacan advances here is a shift away from what is commonly hammered home. There is no escaping this. As for the sexual difference, S_1/S_2, it belongs, according to Lacan, to the symbolic register; it is an effect of metaphor, that is to say an effect of substituting one signifier for another, validated by the grooves of common discourse. In fact, Lacan specifies in, *...or Worse*, that "an organ is an instrument only through the intervention of the fact that it is a signifier, which is what founds any instrument."[3] To say "man" and to define him by an "organ," the penis, is, from then on, only an effect of metaphor.

1. Lacan, J., *Seminar Book XIX*, *...or Worse* (1971-1972), text established by J.-A. Miller, trans. A.R. Price, Cambridge Polity, 2018, p. 28.

2. Lacan, J., Seminaire XXV, "Le moment de conclure" (1977-1978), lesson of 15 November 1977, published under the title "Une pratique de bavardage," *Ornicar ?* 19, 1979, p. 6.

3. Lacan, J., *...or Worse*, *op. cit.*, p. 9.

THE FEMININE OUTSIDE GENDER

Today, this woman/man binary is collapsing. It has been given a pounding by the onward march of recent movements of opinion that have exploded this reduction of the sexual difference by pluralizing the gender categories: LGBTQIA+. In this case too, Lacan turns out to have been able to predict that it is quite possible, and even necessary, to think of sexual difference outside this binary. For we already find the proposal of a third sex in the Seminar, *D'un Autre à l'autre*, and again in a later seminar.

It remains to be seen what Lacan means by this. In this Seminar, he links it to the two sexes, masculine and feminine: "It seems obvious that there are only two, but why shouldn't there be three or more?"[4] In 1979, in "Topology and Time", he comes back to it: "There is no sexual relation, that's what I said. What is there to make up for it? Because it is clear that people—human beings, as we say—make love. There is an explanation for this: the possibility of a third sex—let us note that the possible is what we have defined as that which *stops being written*. Why there are two of them, moreover, is difficult to explain."[5] We will discuss here this act of "making love" and its components: the speaking body and the barred big Other, Ⱥ.

Lacan's capacity to anticipate the evolution of the master's discourses is based on the formalization he makes of the four discourses and of the Borromean knotting.[6]

---

4. Lacan, J., *Seminaire, Livre XVI, D'Un Autre à l'autre* (1968-1969), text established by J.-A. Miller, Paris, Seuil/Champ Freudien, 2006, p. 222.

5. Lacan, J., Le Séminaire, livre XXVI, "La topologie et le temps" (1978-1979), lesson of 9 January 1979, unpublished.

6. Lacan, J., *Seminar XVII, op. cit.,* and *Seminar XXIII, op. cit.*

In this same Seminar, he defines the symbolic through language and its laws, and thus through the quantum of universality.

Gender is an effect of the social bond and of power; it is not a matter of nature. Thanks to scientific advances, gender is no longer at the service of the reproduction of the species. It is necessary to bear this in mind if we wish to approach the feminine position in psychoanalysis. The master's discourses, whether traditional or challenging, have an absolute power on human beings; as speaking subjects, we are an effect of this discourse. As soon as we use the words "woman" or "man", "men" or "women", we reintroduce the categorical logic of the master's discourse of domination, in this case "gendered," and we depart from the logic of the analytic discourse. Gender is linked to saying: *so-called men* and *so-called women*, *so-called gays* and *so-called lesbians*, etc. It universalizes. It is grammatical.

Let us think of Freud and the bipartition he operated in the subjective constitution between identifications, on the one hand, and choice of object, on the other.[7] It follows from this that genders are of the order of identification with master signifiers and are not based on a mode of jouissance.

It is therefore without gender (or genders) that I wish to approach the feminine. For it can be said that the analytic discourse is *a*-gendered—to be understood with equivocation: without gender, but not without the object *a*, not without this object that determines sexual

---

7. Cf. Freud, S., *New Introductory Lectures on Psychoanalysis* (1936), *SE 22*, London, Vintage, 2001. The link between identification and object choice is a red thread running through Freud's work.

preference. It will not be a question here of women or men, but of the feminine, regardless of what gender the subject affirms or subjectivizes. This requires the rigorous discipline of turning the master's discourse inside out—into the analytic discourse.

The Feminine Beyond Fantasy

Whether they are heterosexual or LGBTQIA+, speaking beings share the same form of sexuality: that which is ordered by what Freud brought to light—the fantasy. Thanks to its repetition in several clinical cases, Freud showed that the archetype of the fantasy could be reduced to one sentence. This is the device that allows sexual jouissance regardless of gender. The particularity of this device of jouissance is that it is a sentence or an image with three elements. In the cases studied by Freud, the sentence is, *a child is being beaten*, which knots together these three elements: the one who beats, the one who is beaten and the one who looks on. It thus operates a conjunction between the sadomasochistic drive and the scopic drive in such a way that the speaking body finds itself occupying three places—passive, active and extimate—at the same time.

From this, Lacan produces the algorithm: $\$\Diamond a$. He does this from what he himself qualifies as his invention in psychoanalysis, the object *plus-de-jouir* (surplus jouissance) or object *a*, extricated and defined progressively throughout his teaching. In speaking beings, the fantasy is the key to one of the sexual jouissances. This jouissance is a body event, located in erogenous zones. With or without partner(s), it is fundamentally autoerotic, confirming *that there is no sexual relation*. This jouissance is experienced by all genders—paradoxically, what we find here is a form of the universal.

Encore, Again

Let us go back to *Encore* where we find the Table of Sexuation.[8] This is Lacan's unprecedented innovation not only for the field of psychoanalysis, but for knowledge in general: the abandonment of complementarity between sexual jouissances.

I posit that the so-called masculine side of sexuation is the one where we can place all speaking bodies, "men" in the sense of "human beings." I take up here the neologism LOM, which Lacan, in 1975, uses to designate "LOM, LOM at base, bockedy LOM who's gotta body and Kun have just the one."[9] Let us note that LOM is linked to the speaking body and to existence, to *Yad'lun* [a spoken contraction of *il y a de l'un*, "there is something of the one"] and not to "I am", or to the want-to-be. J.-A. Miller, in his course "The One-all-alone,"[10] put to work this opposition between an ontology and a henology of speaking bodies, between an *I am* and a *there is* that appears in Lacan's very last teaching and which he writes as the neologism, "*Yad'lun.*"[11]

The jouissance on the side of "LOM at base" is organized by these two formulas:

---

8. Lacan, J., *Seminar XX, Encore* (1972-1973), text established by J.-A. Miller, trans. B. Fink, London/New York, Norton, 1998, p. 78-9, reproduced above, see page 16.

9. Lacan, J., "Joyce the Symptom" (1975), trans. A.R. Price, *The Lacanian Review* 5, 2018, pp. 13-18.

10. Miller, J.-A., "L'orientation lacanienne. *L'Un-tout-seul*", *op. cit.*, lesson of 6 April 2011.

11. Lacan, J., *Seminar XIX, ... or Worse, op. cit.*, pp. 109-110, 162-163.

$$\exists x \ \overline{\Phi x} \ // \ \forall x \ \Phi x$$

The first reads, *there exists an x* ($\exists x$) *for which the function phi of x* ($\overline{\Phi x}$) *is negated*. There is an *x* which does not respond to the phallic function, which is to be understood as the function of castration. There is thus an exception to the original loss introduced into the living being by virtue of the fact of being an effect of language. Positing this exception allows the delimitation of a set, of an all, in that it can be negated in its entirety.

The formula, *for all x, phi of x is a universal*: all living beings who speak fall under the domination of the castration function. We therefore have here a jouissance that answers to the homophone of *non* (no) and *Nom* (name) in the *Nom-du-Père* (Name-of-the-Father). This jouissance is Oedipal, as it must first be forbidden in order to be permitted. The castration function, often imaginarized by the confusion of the phallus with the penis, is rather to be strictly defined as a language function. For human beings, there is no access to sexual jouissance without language. The exception of the "one" contained in "there exists one" is the element which, escaping from the set, makes it possible to posit a universal set which is *not* of the register of existence. This set responds to the universality of castration, which is defined as the loss of bodily jouissance implicated by language, speech and discourse. Jouissance is reduced to the linguistic device of the fantasy. It comes to nestle in an object of surplus jouissance, object *a*—the consequence of the subject's inherent want-to-be.

The other side of the Table of Sexuation distinguishes a logical space which is neither complementary to the side called masculine nor reciprocal to it. Lacan describes it as "supplementary." Whereas all the LOMs are on the side called "masculine," not all of them, however, and not all of the time, are on the side of sexuation called "feminine".

$$\overline{\exists}x\ \overline{\Phi}x\ //\ \overline{\forall}x\ \Phi x$$

In Lacan's two formulas—*there does not exist an x for which the function phi of x is negated* and *not all x, phi of x*—the quantums "there exists" and "for all" are negated: this is an invention. Lacan makes it an Other jouissance—$J\not{A}$—the matrix of the side of sexuation called feminine, coming randomly *in addition* to phallic jouissance. "Any speaking being [...] is allowed to inscribe itself in this part,"[12] he emphasizes. It is not a question of dividing men on one side and women on the other as is done in religions, changing rooms or toilets, and more generally in any institutionalized social order. Moreover, with regard to one of his examples of this feminine, Saint John of the Cross, Lacan specifies, "One is not obliged, when one is male, to situate oneself on the side of $\forall x\ \Phi x$."[13] Gender is therefore irrelevant here, as is anatomy. The set in question does not form an *all*; it is open, inconsistent, floating.

It is this so-called feminine side of sexuation of which I now wish to deploy certain clinical modes. I do not claim to give a general illumination of it, as that would be contradictory to the logical space thus defined of the not-all. I will only try to shed light on what seems to me to be a few possible variations of this not-all starting from what is said by analysands.

---

12. Lacan, J., *Encore*, *op. cit.*, p. 80.

13. *Ibid.*, p. 76.

THE HETEROS IN THE WORDS OF ANALYSANDS

Mary Beard, in a recently published short book,[14] evokes silence as having characterized the feminine throughout history. She makes a manifesto of this in a militant and feminist way, of course, so it is not at all the orientation that emerges from the clinical data at work here. Nevertheless, let us keep this point in mind: silence is an important element in the approach to the not-all, a guise of language and speech in the clinical framework.

Freud, in his development of the fantasy, started from the repetition of the same scenario in various subjects. For this research, I base myself on the repetition of similar elements taken from the speech of fifteen subjects in analysis and distilled into four categories (Hiding, Disobedi-sense, Anonymous, Disappearing)—each illustrating modes of supplementary jouissance. Among these fifteen subjects in analysis, two are not mothers. We can therefore assume that the part of the not-all that is involved ex-sists to the position of mother. (On several occasions since 1992, J.-A. Miller has developed the modalities of these two positions: mother and wife[15]—different, they are neither complementary nor antinomic.) These subjects are either married, have a partner, or are single. They speak different languages and come from different cultures. The following are statements extracted from these cures. We will approach them in a Moebian way. Indeed, far from the model of a deep unconscious, the passage from the

14. Beard, M., *Women & Power: A Manifesto*, London, Profile Books, 2017.

15. Miller, J.-A., "Medée à mi-dire" and "Mèrefemme", *La Cause du désir* 89, *op. cit.* pp. 113-14, 115-122.

conscious to the unconscious and back follows the twist of a Moebius strip.

Scattered Signifiers

Certain terms reappear, scattered, in these words that come out of the mouths of different analysands. Their repetition caught my attention and I made a list of them, a swarm, to use Lacan's term—*essaim*—which equivocates with its homonym "S_1" in French, but which also differentiates it: "Analytical theory sees the One rearing its head at two of its levels. At a first level, the One is the One that repeats." At the second level: "The One at issue, which the subject produces—an ideal point, let's say—in analysis, is, contrary to what is at issue in repetition, the One as One by itself."[16] With these examples, we are at the first level of the One.

I use the personal pronoun "she" to indicate that these signifiers arise from a feminine position of jouissance.

Hiding

– She says: "I am talking to a man. He is a writer. Talking with him gives me an incommunicable sense of being understood, as if we understood each other. I don't know why it's so important to do it in secret from everyone, including my husband. It's not a question of sex between us. It's about not doing things clearly, not saying them. It's a matter of secrecy, even for me."

16. Lacan, J., *Seminar XIX, … or Worse, op. cit.* pp. 144-145.

– She says: "It happened to me when I was very young, on holiday with my parents. Meeting an unknown boy in a foreign country. Sneaking away. Meeting him every night, in secret from everyone. Coming home at five in the morning through the window. A satisfaction outside the family, outside the bond, outside time."

– She says: "I'm hiding. It's the same as when I was a teenager, I used to dress in such a way so as to hide my body. I hide myself from sight. What is there to hide? I remember the first novel of my childhood, *Lili and the Secret Testament.*"

Disobedi-sense

– She says: "It's terrible, this inclination to disobey, always a little, whatever the rule, whether I find it just or unjust, necessary or superfluous. Not obeying totally, always a little bending of the rules, known only to me. Most of the time it doesn't really matter. A hidden satisfaction of showing that human law is not the law of gravity. A vague whiff of guilt. It's a pointless satisfaction, really. Even dangerous, sometimes. Or is this what it's about—contravening? I don't understand it at all. How stupid this compulsive disobedience is!"

Anonymous, Outside the Name

– She says: "I was at a weekend work event with my child. When the time came, I went to put him to bed in his room. Then I came back to the meeting. We didn't talk to each other, we went together to his tent. I didn't know his name. We went to bed and got undressed. An event in my body, something I had never experienced before. It lasted for a while. Even though I knew his contact details afterwards, it left me without any particular interest. It was the anonymity itself that was functioning."

– She says: "I had only seen him two or three times. He had caught my eye, but I didn't even know his name. He was a complete stranger. The same attraction, the same satisfaction, but this time a great anxiety."

– She says, "I don't know him, I don't know who he is. He starts sending me increasingly urgent messages. I want him more than anything. I meet him and explain to him that this is not possible. He understands and leaves. I am overcome by a terrible sadness that turns into a panic attack. It is not linked to missing him. It's not because he's gone. When I put my photo on social networks, I know that he sees it when he clicks on it. The anxiety falls away. "Watch where I am [*où je suis*]." I know he follows me [*me suit/suis*]. His gaze has not gone."

– She says: "I went abroad alone when I was twenty years old. I met him in the desert. He invited me to share his house. We lived together for three weeks. I didn't even know his name. Then I returned home to my studies. He was the only great love of my life."

Silence, Outside Speech

– She says: "The important point, I think, is silence. I interpreted silence as a secret. Not to be invaded by words. I made my mother talk all the time in order to avoid her silence."

– She says: "I can't make love with a man who talks. I need silence."

Disappearing

– She says: "From my previous analysis, what remains is the word *discreet*, a discreet woman."

– She says: "The moment I feel someone's authority imposing on me, I make myself disappear. I become unassailable because I have nothing to lose that can be taken away from me. I have another way of existing. This brings me back to a form of solitude. At last it appears. But it doesn't affect my desire, it doesn't prevent me from making myself known, in connection with a lot of people. For example, I was a good student, but I was missing something, a nomination. Hiding."

– She says: "I was looking forward to my analytic session. But in the end, without thinking about it, I took off."

– She says: "Disappearing, not showing myself. Something of the order of erasure. Trying not to be there, trying not to show myself. That's how I chose my partners: to erase myself behind them, so that they take up all the space, a screen of talk. The day of the accident, baby, I was absent from the scene. I wasn't there. Not being exposed to any demonstration of tenderness. Dodging any request and keeping my distance."

– She says: "Put a man in front of me who speaks for me; stay in the shadows."

– She says: "To be in my box. A closed place."

– She says: "I am locked up. A suit of armor."

– She says: "Above all, make me forget."

– She says: "He says to me, 'It's as if you were not there'."

– She says: "A word that constantly comes up as a leitmotif: *soltarse* [Spanish: to come loose]."

– She says: "I've been sleeping since I was little. That's what I like to do the most."

– She says: "In my analysis, I was talking during the sessions, I was in the moment. My analyst chanted, 'Where are you? Where are you?'"

– She says: "No place, nowhere—I just wanted to be a passer-by."

Concerning these signifiers that are repeated, I will bring into play the three dimensions of the imaginary, the symbolic and the real, before inscribing them on a diagram whose form I take from the graphicization constructed by Lacan in *Seminar XX*.[17]

HETEROTISM OR THE EROTISM OF THE VOID

J.-A. Miller emphasizes that Lacan, in his very last teaching, and without denying the incidence of a jouissance linked to the forbidden, "isolated a jouissance that is non-symbolizable, unsayable, having affinities with the infinite,"[18] as in "a whirling geyser of inexhaustible life," a jouissance "outside the signifier," that cannot be said, that is not susceptible to castration; a "jouissance reduced to the body event." Following this orientation, I now propose the term *heterotism*.

The word "hetero" is present in the common discourse and designates, according to the dictionary, a person having sexual preferences for people of the

---

17. Lacan, J., *Seminar XX, Encore*, *op. cit.*, p. 90.

18. Miller, J.-A., "L'orientation lacanienne. *L'Un-tout-seul*", *op. cit.*, lesson of 2 March 2011.

opposite sex. It is an amusing definition that deals with the semantic field of the sexual union; it immediately puts forward the idea of opposition and of conflict between the two sexes. Indeed, in language they are opposed. But here, it suits our purposes to settle on the meaning of the ancient Greek word *heteros*, which means "other,": a *heteros* jouissance, a jouissance other than phallic jouissance, feminine jouissance, an erotism proper to the feminine. As Lacan says in his seminar *Encore*, with regard to she who experiences it, "This jouissance that she is not-all [...] makes her absent from herself somewhere, absent as subject."[19] For all that, this absence from herself does not make her other to her body, for "love, while it is true that it has a relationship with the One, never takes anyone out of themselves."[20] If "being [is] what slips away most in language,"[21] this *absence from herself as a subject* produces an existence in the paradoxical form of a void in the body.

The analysands whose words I have just quoted clearly separate certain experiences of jouissance from other modes of satisfaction—that are nevertheless not foreign to them—a jouissance that imposes itself and makes them absent from themselves, other to themselves. To account for these experiences of jouissance, I propose this diagram of heterotism (see page 52) on which I will now comment.

19. Lacan, J., *Seminar XX, Encore*, *op. cit.*, p. 35.

20. *Ibid.*, p. 47.

21. *Ibid.*, p. 39.

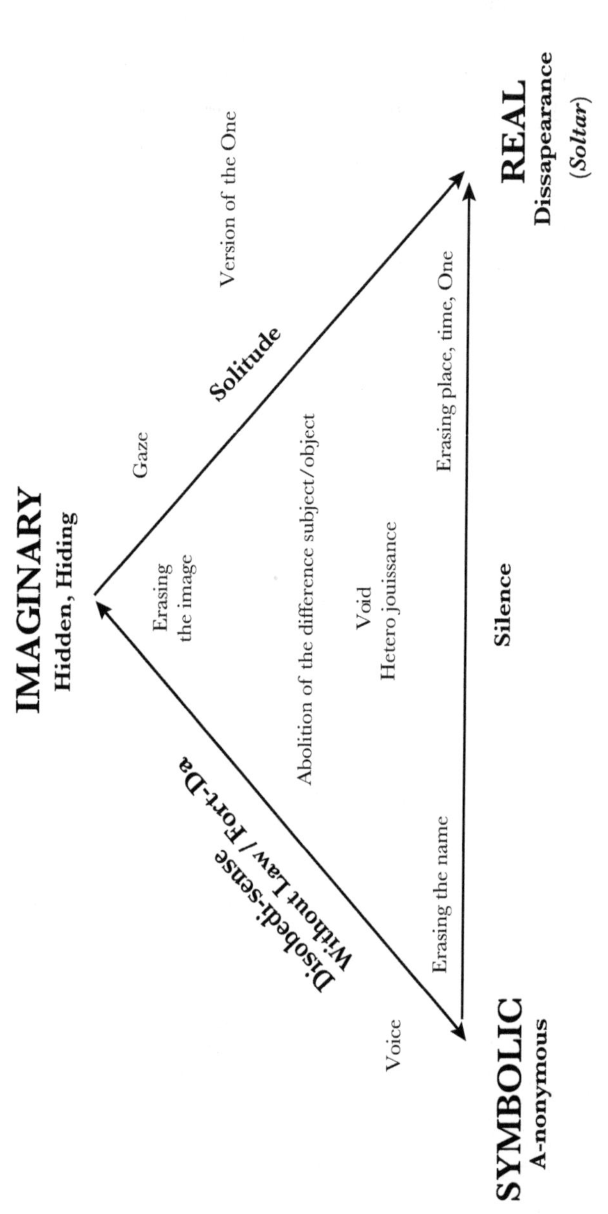

Three Guises of the Void
Not without Φ (castration function)
Not all Φ
IMAGINARY
Hidden, Hiding
Gaze
Erasing
the image
Solitude
Version of the One
REAL
Dissapearance
(Soltar)
Abolition of the difference subject/object
Void
Hetero jouissance
Erasing place, time, One
Silence
Disobedi-sense
Without Law / Fort-Da
Erasing the name
Voice
SYMBOLIC
A-nonymous

Drawing

It is a triangle with three vertices: the imaginary, where seeing and the image prevail, a dimension characterized by its consistency according to Lacan;[22] the symbolic, where the Name and the Law (not without the letter) prevail, a dimension characterized by the hole and relating to the object voice; the real, without law and without image, a dimension that ex-sists to the other two dimensions on condition that "it encounters, with the symbolic and the imaginary, a point of arrest."[23] Thinking about the real requires this ex-sisting.

To these three vertices, I have associated signifiers that were repeated in the words of different analysands, all of whom fall within the neurotic structure. *Hiding* for the imaginary, *anonymous* for the symbolic and *disappearance* for the real which is a black hole. The sides of the triangle have been transformed into vectors. On the imaginary-symbolic vector I have put the equivocation disobedience/disobedi-sense. This follows the RSI[24] diagram commented on by Lacan in *The Sinthome*, since it situates meaning between the ring of the imaginary and the ring of the symbolic. It is on this vector that I have also placed the *Fort-Da*, which is the matrix for all separation in language, brought to light by Freud in *Beyond the Pleasure Principle.*

The other two vectors are univocal because they only refer to the real in which they find their point of arrest.

---

22. Cf. Lacan, J., *Seminar XXIII, The Sinthome*, *op. cit.* p. 38: "It is not by chance [...] that I place in the imaginary this support of what makes for consistency."

23. *Ibid.*

24. *Ibid.*, p. 42.

On the vector from the symbolic towards the real, silence (which is there a form of speech) runs as a symptomatic modality, and on the vector from the imaginary towards the real, I place solitude as the symptomatic modality. When the imaginary prevails, to be the only one is interpreted as being the one and only for another. But the more solitude approaches the real, the more the semblable is erased, and here, solitude takes the value of the One. In his seminar *D'un Autre à l'autre*, Lacan spends several sessions mobilizing his set theory in order to consider imagining the one without the two. J.-A. Miller shed light on this process by entitling these two chapters, "The Logical Genesis of Surplus Jouissance" and "Concerning One More."[25]

At the imaginary vertex, an erasing of the image is aimed at; at the symbolic vertex, an erasing of the Name; at the real vertex, an erasing of the One. I will come back to these erasings.

Within the triangle, I have situated the emptiness obtained in these three ways. An emptiness that I characterize as being the aim of an abolition of the subject/object difference by the parlêtre. An emptiness that is a kind of disengagement from the mechanism of effectuation of the subject that constitutes the pair "alienation-separation," the parlêtre's fundamental mode of causation.[26]

25. Lacan, J., *Seminar XVI, D'un Autre à l'autre*, *op. cit.*, chap. 23 and 24, pp. 355 and 375.

26. Lacan, J., "Position of the Unconscious", *Écrits*, *op. cit.*, p. 711 *et seq.*

Of the Void

As I have said before, ever since J.-A. Miller's work on the theses of J.-P. Changeux—which enabled Changeux to find the title of his book *Neuronal Man* in 1983—our working community has lacked data on the progress of science. My meeting with two physicists, which I mentioned in the introduction, taught me how the notion of the void is central to the problems of current physics.

Epistemologically speaking, we know that concepts are capable of passing from one discipline to another. Can the concept of the void be of interest to psychoanalysis? I think so. Freud had difficulty when he characterized female sexuality as the "dark continent"[27] within the discipline he had just founded. One could say that it is the black hole of Freudian psychoanalysis. Since then, and in spite of Lacan's lightning advances, few works, as even he noted on many occasions, have been produced on this question. Considering this, it is interesting for us to see if the concepts of "void" and "gravitational waves" generated by the destruction of black holes can, when plunged into and used in the analytic experience, produce effects of knowledge.

Can jouissance on the side of the not-all (the feminine side of sexuation) find in the void a formulation that would allow us to know a little more? The void is both a void of matter (that of the matter of fantasy) and a mass of energy (that of the Other jouissance: JȺ) that inhabits the speaking body at certain moments. Lacan defines the materiality of the body by its consistency.[28] Is it of the

27. Freud, S., "The Question of Lay Analysis" (1926), *SE* Vol. 20, p. 212.

28. Cf. Lacan, J., *Seminar XXIII, The Sinthome, op. cit.*, p. 38.

order of an energy without specific localization in any organ of the body, an energy that seizes the speaking body as *One* in its global existence? This is the path I am taking here, guided by the words of analysands: to put to the psychoanalytic test the void as ex-sistence of a jouissance delocalized with respect to the orificial zones invested by the fantasy. This does not mean that it abolishes them. These experiences, which always surprise the speakers when they occur, are not without bringing objects *a* into play, but are not reproducible from the formula of a fantasy and do not mobilize a precise erogenous zone. The effect is diffuse, delocalized.

Erasings of the Image, the Name, and the One

Let us go further. Certain objects *a* come into play here, in a very particular mode. They fade away to make room for a subjective disappearance that is the key to this other, non-localizable satisfaction.

Recently rereading the seminar *D'un Autre à l'autre*, some colleagues and I were again surprised by the formulation, "the four erasings of the subject,"[29] designating the objects *a* in play. I have been inspired by Lacan's creation of the term "erasings" in the little diagram I propose here. A few years earlier, in Baltimore in 1966, during an international meeting on structuralism, Lacan had already formulated it in this way: "Where is the subject? It is necessary to find the subject as a lost object. More

---

29. Lacan, J., *Séminaire,* livre XVI, *D'un Autre à l'autre, op. cit.*, p. 314 *et seq*. [TN: In French, the phrase is, "*les quatre éffaçons du sujet.*" The word "*effaçons*" means "let's erase," but here is used as a noun, "erasings." In the pun "*l'effaçon*" (Lacan, J., "Radiophonie," *Autres écrits*, Paris, Seuil, 2001, p. 427) we hear the homophone, "*les façons,*" or "the ways."]

precisely this lost object is the support of the subject and in many cases is a more abject thing than you may care to consider."[30] With regard to the sameness of the mark, i.e. the unary trait, he adds, "the subject is here, [...] in this obscure thing."[31]

At the three vertices of the triangle there is indeed a process that erases the image, the name and the One.

Hiding is a mode of satisfaction set up as a game by children, such as "peekaboo." This is a game about the disappearance of an image, particularly a self-image. This satisfaction is part of the logic of the *Fort-Da*, highlighted by Freud in his study of the child's game of making a cotton-reel appear and disappear.[32] In this appearance/disappearance, the symbolic—in its function both as letter and as encryption—is part of the game thanks to the hole that makes the signifying chain possible. It is both as letter and as encryption that the erasing performs—as the trait or mark that is the name. As I write these lines, I am thinking of the writer Romain Gary who, breaking the law of the Goncourt Prize, managed to obtain it twice under two different names: Gary and Ajar. This was less a maneuver than a monstration of the futility of the proper name to measure up to writing with someone whose proper name was not even "Gary." Names, since they can be changed, invented, given or chosen, have no hold on the referent, which remains out of reach except via the object through

30. See Lacan, J., "Of Structure as an Inmixing of an Otherness Prerequisite to Any Subject Whatever" *The Lacanian Review* 12, 2021, pp. 20-34.

31. *Ibid.*, p. 192.

32. Freud, S., "Beyond the Pleasure Principle" (1920), *SE* 18, *op. cit.*, pp. 1-64.

unconscious desire. Psychoanalysis chooses to deal only with what holds as a reference point for the parlêtre, that is to say, with *motérialité*. The referent is the word [*mot*] as sound matter, implying the fall of meaning.

Finally, disappearance is an erasing of the division that returns within the death drive. It is a letting-go—which is a condition of a jouissance. But it is not without the imaginary of the hiding place, characterized in the words quoted earlier of the analysands who spoke of "bubble" and "box." It is a mixture of box and refuge, an impossible place: a sort of *there's someone*, or even *there's no one*, or *there's nothing* [*y'a quelqu'un, y'a personne, y'a rien*], here echoing J.-A. Miller's invention, *There's a bit o'woman here* [*Ici y'a d'la femme*] in "Médée à mi-dire."[33]

It is an impossible: to be other to oneself—"*otra a si misma*," said one analysand. It is not a question here of the Other woman dear to the hysterical structure, but of the barred Other essential to the feminine, $\cancel{A}$. I am thinking of Lacan's phrase in the seminar *Encore*: "To realize that love, while it is true that it has a relationship with the One, never makes anyone leave himself behind."[34] Lacan's invention, which takes him beyond the Freudian discovery of the narcissistic nature of love, appears in the equivoque of loving oneself [*s'aimer*] and "saming" oneself [the neologism *se mêmer*][35] in the Other that is not. The expression, "We love each other," subject to the equivoque in French ("we 'same' [*s'aime*] each other"), highlights the lovingness and the sameness that are key here: I love you because you are the same as me.

---

33. Miller, J.-A., "Médée à mi-dire," *op. cit.*, p. 113.
34. Lacan, J., *Seminar XX, Encore, op. cit.*, p. 47.
35. Cf. *ibid.*, p. 85, fn. 23.

But "to the extent that they are the same in the Other," an impasse arises, as Lacan points out, because "there is no need to know you are Other to be there."[36]

Note that Lacan's formulation has infiltrated current discourse; to be the same in the Other has entered the social bond through the internet practice of "memes," which produces an effect of non-sense by operating small variations in an image or a word. Feminization?

Disobedi-sense and Silence

As Lacan says in his seminar *The Sinthome*, "Meaning emanates from a field that lies between the imaginary and the symbolic. That goes without saying."[37] Here we find a relationship to the law that reveals it as nothing more than an artifice of the name, traditionally unfavorable to human beings called women. To escape the fragility of names and the fluidity of images: blank slate. This explains the imperative of silence according to Mary Beard, but also the imperative of a word that neither names nor counts (in both senses of the word): *chattering*, a term traditionally used to describe those who are gendered as women, and which becomes, once turned around, a solution. For there is no such thing as a proper name. As Lacan said about James Joyce, when you want to make a proper name for yourself, you only end up making this a part of the common name.

Silence thus becomes *keeping quiet*. It is no longer an imperative, an order from the Other. It is a radical choice, an erasing from the Other, even an oblivion.

---

36. *Ibid.*

37. Lacan, J., *Seminar XXIII, The Sinthome, op. cit.*, p. 57.

Solitude and Disappearance

I mentioned above the difficulty of imagining the One—the One-all-alone—without ordinal or cardinal numeration. I recalled the titles given by J.-A. Miller to the chapters devoted to the One in the seminar, *D'un Autre à l'autre*: "The Logical Genesis of the Surplus Jouissance" and "Concerning One More." The objective is to make time, which is unmeasurable, coincide with these modalities of the One. But by abolishing the want-to-be that defines and divides the subject, we only end up trying to find a being of object: inert. The mystical solution is not far away, but it requires an Other, a God. Narcissus's solution is, as we know, deadly. So, it concerns rather a disappearance, a *soltarse* in Spanish, a letting-go, a void of thoughts, words, and sensation.

Virginia Woolf wrote a beautiful book called *A Room of One's Own*, but there ex-sists no room that can shelter this self.

JOUISSANCE OF DISAPPEARANCE: TO BE BARRED

Lacan discusses the different modes of jouissance in the chapter entitled, "On the Knot as the Subject's Support" in his seminar *The Sinthome*. He differentiates between phallic jouissance, which is the covering of the symbolic by the real; *meaning*, which is a jouissance coming from the covering of the imaginary by the symbolic; and the *jouissance of the barred Other*, which comes from covering the real by the imaginary.

Lacan also distinguishes phallic jouissance from organ jouissance ("penile jouissance", to which we add clitoral jouissance): organ jouissance "arises in relation to the imaginary, that is, the jouissance of the double, of the specular image, the jouissance of the imaginary body." And, he continues, organ jouissance "constitutes the different objects that occupy the gaps of which the body is the imaginary support."[38] I will add that it does not constitute them without the fantasy and therefore not without phallic jouissance.

Lacan then specifies what phallic jouissance is: "Phallic jouissance is, however, located here at the conjunction between the symbolic and the real. This is so to the extent that, in the subject who is supported by the parlêtre, which is what I denote as the unconscious, we find *might*, which is called upon and sustained to conjoin a certain jouissance that, due to the fact of this very speech, conjoins with so-called phallic jouissance. Phallic jouissance is experienced, given the fact of the parlêtre, as parasitic [...] I am writing this phallic jouissance here, thus balancing out what is involved in meaning. This is the locus of that which in consciousness is denoted by the parlêtre as *might*." We thus see that organ jouissance, phallic jouissance and jouissance of meaning are knotted in the parlêtre.

What remains is JȺ, *the jouissance of the barred Other*, between real and imaginary, the one that is aimed at in the schema I am proposing, that of the disappearance of the erasing—impossible. What does Lacan say about JȺ? "This barred A means that there is no Other of the Other, that is to say, nothing stands in opposition to the symbolic, the locus of the Other as such. Thus, there is no jouissance

38. *Ibid.*, pp. 43-44, *et seq.*

of the Other, because there is no Other of the Other. The result of this is that the jouissance of the Other of the Other is not possible for the simple reason that there is none."

So how do we think about these subjective experiences that analysands share? How do we name these modalities of the erasing of the image, the name, the place, the time, and the One? Let us return to *Encore*.

It is not a question of a jouissance of an Other that would be beyond the Other of the symbolic and the imaginary. The jouissance written as JȺ by Lacan is a jouissance located in the bar on the Other as in the bar on "~~Woman~~," this Woman of the universal which, in this place, does not exist. This ~~Woman~~ cannot be said when it is a question of "a supplementary jouissance," a jouissance that is not all phallic. Lacan states it thus: *~~Woman~~ does not exist*; "Woman can only be written with a bar through it." And he specifies: "I already spoke of man (*l'homme*) and the 'woman' (la *femme*). That 'woman' (*la*) is a signifier. With it I symbolize the signifier whose place it is indispensable to mark—that place cannot be left empty."[39]

In both cases, the bar is the effect of the cancellation of the quantifier: *It exists*, quantifier of existence, and *For-all*, quantifier of the universal. The cancellation of the existence quantifier, $\exists$, refers us to the famous sentence from *Oedipus at Colonus*, "It would be better not to have been born." In other words, it refers us to the power of the Freudian death drive, which Lacan makes the definition of any drive. As for the quantifier of universality, $\forall$, it relates to saying and thus to the world of language as

39. Lacan, J., *Seminar XX, Encore, op. cit.*, pp. 72-73.

the fiction that constitutes the fabric of reality in which humans evolve. It guarantees the domain of meaning and imposes the imperative. Its negation does not produce nonsense and anarchy, but opens an unknown space-time, an inconsistent place.

What is left then? Certainly, there remains the object *a*, but separated from the formula of the fantasy and without connection with the divided subject. "Something other than object *a* is at stake in what comes to make up for (*suppléer*) the sexual relationship that does not exist."[40] What is it then? If it is not A, and if it is not *a*, there remains the subject, on the one hand, and, on the other, the bar itself which can function as an object: S and A have the bar in common. Let us therefore posit that this jouissance of disappearance in its different forms—imaginary (hidden from the Other), symbolic (anonymous, i.e. without a name in the Other) and real (disappearance of the subject into a One)—what I have pinned on the term "*erasing*," borrowed from Lacan, is the jouissance of the bar itself which affects not the parlêtre, but the speaking body. It is a question of making oneself a bar, of barring oneself.

There is therefore a jouissance in "being barred": being barred from the all, but not completely, not all the time. This echoes an equivoque of Lacan's about subjects who precisely do not allow themselves to be grasped in any *all*: not mad-at-all—"not-at-all-mad-about-the-whole (*folles-de-tout*)."[41] This is amusing, since the term is also used in colloquial French: "*T'es complètement barré(e)!*"—"You're out of your mind!"

40. *Ibid.*, p. 63.

41. Cf. Lacan, J., "Television", *op. cit.*, p. 40.

Let us return for a moment to the master's discourse on women: their exclusion from the City and its various economic and political mechanisms; their confinement to the house or to women's quarters; their assignment to the maternal function or to domestic work, carried out by tradition—all these are barriers. These different barriers are then turned into a mode of enjoying the bar itself: *You want me to be an object, you want me to be silent, you think I'm not human, you think me a womb to procreate your lineage, a parlêtre outside the for-all? Well, okay then, I'll be the bar itself—for a moment, unlocatable, neither to you nor to myself, radically other:* heteros.

This not-all phallic solution (which does not mean not at all phallic), which produces the void in the subject, is not, however, without objects. But the connection of the objects to the want-to-be, and thus to their function as cause of desire, has changed. This solution no longer responds solely, in certain circumstances, to the modality of necessity; it obeys the contingency of encounters, good or bad. The not-all is in harmony with the *tyché*.

This *becoming the bar* evokes the cut. This anonymity evokes the reduction of the name to the letter. So many points which are not without evoking the end of analysis and the passage to the analyst. What remains of the analysand that was? Disappeared? Hidden in love for psychoanalysis? Or anonymous? Reduced to the letter?

CONCLUSION

In 1955, well before advancing the logic of sexuation in *Encore*, Lacan, returning to Freud's death drive, said, "Oedipean psychoanalysis is achieved only at Colonus." Strange place, Colonus. Driven out of Thebes and wandering for years on the roads with his daughter, Oedipus arrived in Colonus where sacred and profane spaces merged; a border place. As I write these lines, I cannot help but think of those called "migrants" wandering the world in this 21st century. But Colonus is also the place where Oedipus disappeared without it being possible to say what happened to him. The final scene of Sophocles' last tragedy shows Oedipus vanishing into thin air, disappearing into a black hole, into the void. He became pure energy, and his tomb is still hidden.

Passing from analysand to analyst is to mobilize the logic of the not-all, a plunge into the unknown. Homophonic in the French, you may read this as you will: "un" or "One."

In fact, it is a matter of agreeing to occupy that place which J.-A. Miller, in his 2007-2008 course, characterized as the *place de plus personne*—the place of no-one-anymore. The void, the null, which I have made use of in this book, can be found in the term *nullibiété*,[1] a neologism[2] of Lacan that J.-A. Miller actualized and recognized as the place of no-one-anymore. He reworked the negation of the quantum of universality, "this special quantum" $\overline{\forall}$ and affirmed, "There is nothing universal about the analytic discourse." As J.-A. Miller pointed out, Lacan's statement[3] refers to the status he gives to the feminine, to feminine sexuation built on the negated *for-all x*, that is, on the not-all. Noting here that truth is related to jouissance, he proposed, "The truth says of itself *je me démens, je démens, je me défile, je me défends*—I'm ducking, I'm dodging, I'm flitting, I'm fending off." There where the no-one-anymore is—in this supplementary, random and inconsistent zone—subjective truth changes status, as does the unconscious: it becomes pure *motérialité* emptied of meaning in part by its equivoque; silence and words slide towards a void. This void is the black hole of the body event.

1. Miller J.-A., "L'orientation lacanienne. Tout le monde est fou", *op. cit.*

2. Cf. Lacan, J., *Le Séminaire*, livre XVI, *D'un Autre à l'autre*, *op. cit.*, p. 327 : "[*nullibiété* …which designates the quality of that which is nowhere." ["*nullibiété* [...] qui désigne la qualité de ce qui n'est nulle part."]

3. Cf. Lacan J., "Journal d'*Ornicar ?* Lacan pour Vincennes !", *op. cit.*

BIBLIOGRAPHY

BARSUGLIA, M., BROUSSE, M.-H., AND MABILLE, D., "The Real and the Metaphoric in Physics," *The Lacanian Review* 7, Spring 2019, pp. 14-27.

BROUSSE, M.-H., DE GEORGES, P., AND PÉPIN, C., "The Perfection of the Void," *The Lacanian Review* 7, Spring 2019, pp. 28-50.

BEARD, M., *Women & Power: A Manifesto,* London, Profile Books, 2017.

CHANGEUX, J.-P., "*L'Homme neuronal*" (1978), interview with J. Bergès, A. Grosrichard, É. Laurent and J.-A. Miller, in *Foucault, Duby, Dumézil, Changeux, Thom. Cinq grands entretiens au Champ freudien,* Paris, Navarin, 2021.

CHENG, F., "François Cheng et Jacques Lacan," *L'Âne* 4, February-March 1982.

FREUD, S.,

"Leonardo Da Vinci and a Memory of His Childhood" (1910), *SE* 11, pp. 59-138.

"The Question of Lay Analysis" (1926), *SE* 20.

"Beyond the Pleasure Principle" (1920), *SE* 18.

New Introductory Lectures on Psychoanalysis (1936), *SE* 22, London, Vintage, 2001.

LACAN, J.,

"The Family Complexes" (1938), trans. A. Khan, *Critical Texts* 53, 1988.

"The Mirror Stage as Formative of the *I* Function as Revealed in Psychoanalytic Experience" (1949), *Écrits*, trans. B. Fink, London/New York, Norton, 2006, pp. 75-81.

"The Function and Field of Speech and Language in Psychoanalysis" (1953), *Écrits*, *op. cit.*, pp. 197-268.

Transference: The Seminar of Jacques Lacan, Book VIII (1960-1961), text established by J.-A. Miller, trans. B. Fink, Cambridge, Polity, 2015.

Le Séminaire, livre IX, "L'identification" (1961- 1962), lesson of 30 May 1962 (unpublished).

Anxiety: The Seminar of Jacques Lacan, Book X (1962-1963), text established by J.-A. Miller, trans. A.R. Price, Cambridge, Polity, 2014.

"Position of the Unconscious" (1964), *Écrits*, *op. cit.*

"Of Structure as an Inmixing of an Otherness Prerequisite to Any Subject Whatever" (1966), *The Lacanian Review* 12, 2021, pp. 20-34.

Écrits: The First Complete Edition in English (1966), trans. B. Fink, London/New York, Norton, 2006.

"Note on the Father and Universalism" (1968), trans. R. Grigg, *The Lacanian Review* 3, 2017.

Séminaire, livre XVI, D'Un Autre à l'autre (1968-1969), text established by J.-A. Miller, Paris, Seuil/Champ Freudien, 2006.

The Other Side of Psychoanalysis: The Seminar of Jacques Lacan, Book XVII (1969-1970), text established by J.-A. Miller, trans. R. Grigg, London/New York, Norton, 1991.

... Or Worse: The Seminar of Jacques Lacan, Book XIX (1971-1972), text established by J.-A. Miller, trans. A.R. Price, Cambridge Polity, 2018.

Encore, On Feminine Sexuality, the Limits of Love and Knowledge: The Seminar of Jacques Lacan, Book XX (1972-1973), text established by J.-A. Miller, trans. B. Fink, London/New York, Norton, 1998.

Le Séminaire, livre XXI, "Les non-dupes errent" (1973-1974), lesson of 19 March 1974 (unpublished).

"Television" (1974), trans. D. Hollier, R. Krauss and A. Michelson, in *Television: A Challenge to the Psychoanalytic Establishment*, ed. J. Copjec, London/New York, Norton, 1990.

Le Séminaire, livre XXII, "R.S.I." (1974-1975), lesson of 21 January 1975, *Ornicar ?* 3, May 1975.

"Geneva Lecture on the Symptom" (1975), trans. R. Grigg, *Analysis* 1, 1989, p. 14.

"Yale University, Kanzer Seminar, 24 November 1975," trans. Philip Dravers, *The Lacanian Review* 12, 2021, pp. 35-57.

"MIT Lecture on Topology, 2 December 1975," trans. J.W. Stone and R. Grigg, *The Lacanian Review* 12, 2021, pp. 78-86.

"Joyce the Symptom" (1975), trans. A.R. Price, *The Lacanian Review* 5, 2018.

The Sinthome: The Seminar of Jacques Lacan, Book XXIII, (1975-1976), text established by J.-A. Miller, trans. A.R. Price, Cambridge, Polity, 2016.

Le Séminaire, livre xxv, "Le moment de conclure" (1977-1978), lesson of 15 November 1977, published under the title "Une pratique de bavardage," *Ornicar ?* 19, 1979.

"There Are Four Discourses" (1978), trans. A.R. Price with R. Grigg, *Culture/Clinic* 1, Minneapolis/London, University of Minnesota Press, 2013, pp. 3-4.

Le Séminaire, livre XXVI, "La topologie et le temps" (1978-1979), lesson of 9 January 1979 (unpublished).

MILLER, J.-A.,

"Médée à mi-dire" (1992), *La Cause du désir* 89, March 2015, p. 114.

"Mèrefemme" (1994), *La Cause du désir* 89, *op. cit.*, p. 122.

"L'orientation lacanienne: *Silet*" (1994-1995), teaching delivered within the framework of the Department of Psychoanalysis at the University of Paris 8 (unpublished).

"L'orientation lacanienne: *Le tout dernier Lacan*" (2006-2007), teaching delivered within the framework of the Department of Psychoanalysis at the University of Paris 8, lesson of 9 May 2007 (unpublished).

"L'orientation lacanienne: *Tout le monde est fou*" (2007-2008), teaching delivered within the framework of the

Department of Psychoanalysis at the University of Paris 8, lesson of 11 June 2008 (unpublished). See also lesson from 4 June 2008, published in English as "Everyone Is Mad", *Culture/Clinic* 1, Minneapolis/London, University of Minnesota Press, 2013, pp. 17-42.

"L'orientation lacanienne: *L'Un-tout-seul*" (2010-2011), teaching delivered within the framework of the Department of Psychoanalysis at the University of Paris 8 (unpublished).

"Bourdin, l'Homme pulsionnel", *Lacan Quotidien* 485, 6 March 2015, available online at lacanquotidien.fr

WAJCMAN, G., *L'Œil absolu*, Paris, Denoël, 2010.

INDEX

Acknowledgements

I must thank Christiane Alberti, my first reader, for her invaluable advice.

My thanks also to Patricia Cagnet, whose design skills greatly aid my theoretical elaborations.

This book would not have seen the light of day without the ongoing conversations I have had with Ève Miller-Rose. I thank her for her determination.

Marie-Hélène Brousse

I would like to thank Pamela King for her careful reading of this translation and also those others who have helped along the way. It's a pleasure to be part of this international network of eager readers, a network that plays a vital role in bringing these ideas to the English-speaking spaces of the world.

Janet Rachel

About the Author

Marie-Hélène Brousse is a psychoanalyst and a university lecturer. She holds a PhD in psychoanalysis and is a Member of the École de la Cause freudienne, New Lacanian School, and the World Association of Psychoanalysis. She has written many papers in the Lacanian Orientation on the subject of motherhood and femininity, translated in several languages. Brousse is the editor in chief of *The Lacanian Review.*

World Association of Psychoanalysis

Libretto series

wapol.org

About the *Libretto* series

Libretto is the book series of the World Association of Psychoanalysis created in 2021 with the Lacanian Press: the first of its kind in English.

It aims at introducing a new presence of what Jacques-Alain Miller has named the "Lacanian Orientation" in the English-speaking world, inviting readers to encounter or re-encounter Lacan's teaching in a lively and serious way.

Lacan's teaching, continuously derived from his *praxis*, offers key concepts for clinicians and practitioners. His elaborations on the "speaking body" are also an essential source for understanding and appreciating contemporary debates concerning human experience and the logics at stake therein.

In this series, members of the World Association of Psychoanalysis will explore the consequences of Freud's discovery of the unconscious and of "Civilisation and Its Discontents" for our times.

The *Libretto* book series will be a central reference point for anybody wishing to engage with Lacanian psychoanalysis which privileges a constantly renewed interpretation of the world we inhabit.

Books in this series will be of interest to psychoanalysts, as well as a wide variety of professionals and students within a diverse range of other disciplines, such as cultural studies, psychology, philosophy, anthropology, psychiatry, biology, genetics, social science, education, literature, and the arts.

About Lacanian Press

Lacanian Press is the publishing house of Lacanian Compass, a group dedicated to the promotion of the Lacanian Orientation of psychoanalysis in the United States and within the English language. Lacanian Compass is an associated group of the New Lacanian School and the World Association of Psychoanalysis. It aims to develop psychoanalysis as first described by Sigmund Freud and elaborated by Jacques Lacan and Jacques-Alain Miller.

lacaniancompass.com

CPSIA information can be obtained
at www.ICGtesting.com
Printed in the USA
BVHW052156030323
659695BV00022B/275